CHILDren's BOOK marKeTING ✨ Magic ✨

SOCIaL MEDIa STraTEGIES FOR CHILDREN'S AUTHORS

WWW.SLOTHDREAMSBOOKS.COM

Text Copyright 2024 by KeriAnne N. Jelinek
Published by Sloth Dreams Books & Publishing, LLC.
Sloth Dreams Marketing Books
Pennsylvania, USA
www.SlothDreamsBooks.com

ISBN: 978-4-5156-5225-1

Children's BOOK Marketing Magic

Social Media Strategies for Children's Authors

KeriAnne Jelinek

Bestselling Children's Author

TABLE OF CONTENT

CHAPTER 1:

INTRODUCTION

Unlock the secrets of successful book promotion with "Children's Book Marketing Magic: Social Media Strategies for Children's Authors." This comprehensive guide provides expert insights and practical tips on leveraging social media to connect with young readers and boost book sales.

From crafting engaging posts to building a strong online presence, discover how to captivate audiences and grow your children's book brand. Don't miss out on this essential resource for authors aiming to make a splash in the competitive world of children's literature. In today's digital age, social media has become an indispensable tool for authors looking to promote their work and engage with their audience.

For children's authors, the power of social media cannot be underestimated. Platforms like Facebook, Instagram, Twitter, and TikTok offer unique opportunities to connect with young readers, parents, and educators in a fun and interactive way. Creating a successful social media strategy requires more than just posting about your book. It's about building a community around your brand, sparking conversations, and fostering relationships with your audience.

By understanding the preferences and behaviors of your target audience, you can tailor your content to resonate with them and keep them coming back for more. One of the key advantages of social media marketing is its ability to level the playing field for authors, allowing even self-published writers to reach a global audience. With the right approach, you can amplify your reach, drive engagement, and ultimately increase book sales.

In this book, we will explore the various social media platforms available to children's authors and delve into strategies for creating compelling and shareable content. We will discuss the importance of visual storytelling, the art of crafting captivating captions, and the value of engaging with your audience in a meaningful way. Whether you're a seasoned author or just starting out, "Children's Book Marketing Magic" will equip you with the knowledge and tools needed to navigate the ever-evolving landscape of social media marketing. So, get ready to unleash the magic of social media and take your children's book marketing to new heights.

Chapter 2:

Understanding Your Audience

Understanding your audience is key to effective marketing in the realm of children's books. When it comes to promoting your work to young readers, it's essential to have a deep understanding of who your target audience is. Children are a unique demographic with specific needs, interests, and behaviors that differ from adults.

To successfully market your children's book on social media, you must first identify and connect with your audience in a meaningful way.

One crucial aspect of understanding your audience is recognizing the age range of the children you are targeting. Different age groups have varying reading preferences and levels of comprehension.

Tailoring your social media content to suit the developmental stage of your audience will ensure that your message resonates with them effectively. Whether you are writing picture books for preschoolers or middle-grade novels for older children, adapting your marketing strategies to cater to the specific age group will help you create content that speaks directly to your readers.

In addition to age considerations, it's essential to understand the interests and hobbies of children within your target audience.

What themes or topics resonate with them? Are there specific genres or characters that capture their imagination? By delving into the interests of your young readers, you can tailor your social media content to align with what appeals to them most. Incorporating elements that speak to their passions and curiosities will make your book marketing efforts more engaging and relevant.

Furthermore, grasping the online behaviors of children and their parents can provide valuable insights into how to effectively reach and engage with them on social media platforms. Understanding which platforms are popular among your target audience and how they interact with content online will help you tailor your marketing strategies for maximum impact.

Whether it's creating interactive posts on Instagram, hosting live storytelling sessions on Facebook, or utilizing educational content on YouTube, knowing where and how to connect with young readers is essential for building a strong online presence. By understanding your audience on a deeper level, you can create authentic and compelling social media strategies that resonate with young readers and drive book sales.

Remember, successful children's book marketing goes beyond simply promoting your work – it's about building meaningful connections with your audience and fostering a community of young readers who are excited to engage with your books.

Embrace the magic of social media and connect with your audience in a way that captivates their hearts and minds.

CHaPTer 3:
CraFTing engaging social Media POSTS

In today's digital age, social media has become a powerful tool for children's authors to reach their target audience and create a lasting impact. Crafting engaging social media posts is not just about promoting your book; it's about building a community of young readers who are excited to engage with your content.

When creating social media posts for your children's book, it's essential to keep your audience in mind. Children have short attention spans, so your posts need to be visually appealing, fun, and easy to digest.

Incorporating colorful graphics, interactive elements, and playful language can help capture the attention of young readers and keep them coming back for more.

One effective strategy for crafting engaging social media posts is to tell stories. Children love stories, so why not use your social media platform to share snippets of your book, behind-the-scenes moments, or even personal anecdotes that relate to your writing journey?

By weaving narratives into your posts, you can create a connection with your audience and make your content more relatable and engaging.

Another important aspect of creating engaging social media posts is to encourage interaction. Pose questions, run polls, or host contests to get children involved and excited about your book. By fostering a sense of community and inviting feedback, you can turn passive followers into active participants who feel personally invested in your work.

Consistency is key when it comes to crafting engaging social media posts. Develop a content calendar and stick to a regular posting schedule to keep your audience engaged and coming back for more.

Whether it's sharing book updates, sneak peeks, or fun facts, make sure your content is relevant, timely, and aligned with your brand. Utilize the features and tools available on different social media platforms to enhance the engagement of your posts.

From Instagram stories to Facebook live sessions, explore creative ways to connect with your audience and bring your children's book to life in the digital realm.

In conclusion, crafting engaging social media posts is a vital component of promoting your children's book and connecting with young readers. By focusing on visual appeal, storytelling, interaction, consistency, and creativity, you can effectively captivate your audience and grow your children's book brand through social media. Embrace the magic of social media marketing and watch your book soar to new heights.

CHAPTER 4:

BUILDING A STRONG ONLINE PRESENCE

In today's digital age, building a strong online presence is crucial for children's authors looking to promote their books and connect with young readers. The power of social media cannot be underestimated when it comes to reaching a wide audience and engaging with your target demographic.

In this chapter, we will delve into the strategies and techniques that will help you establish a compelling online presence that resonates with your audience and drives book sales. One of the first steps in building a strong online presence is to identify your target audience.

Understanding who your readers are and where they spend their time online is essential for crafting a successful social media strategy. Are you writing for young children, middle-grade readers, or young adults?

Tailoring your content to suit the interests and preferences of your audience will help you create engaging posts that resonate with them. Once you have defined your target audience, it's time to choose the right social media platforms to reach them. Each platform has its unique strengths and demographics, so it's important to select the ones that align with your audience and goals.

Whether you choose to focus on platforms like Instagram for visually appealing content, Twitter for real-time updates, or Facebook for building a community around your books, consistency is key.

Crafting engaging posts that capture the attention of young readers is essential for building a strong online presence. Visual content such as eye-catching graphics, videos, and illustrations can help make your posts stand out in a crowded social media landscape.

Share behind-the-scenes glimpses of your writing process, sneak peeks of upcoming projects, or fun facts about your characters to keep your audience engaged and excited about your books.

In addition to creating compelling content, engaging with your audience is crucial for building a strong online presence. Respond to comments, messages, and mentions promptly to show your readers that you value their feedback and are actively listening to their thoughts. Encourage user-generated content by running contests, polls, or challenges that invite your audience to participate and interact with your brand. Consistency is key when it comes to maintaining a strong online presence.

Regularly posting content, interacting with your audience, and staying true to your brand voice will help you establish credibility and build a loyal following. Remember that building a strong online presence is a marathon, not a sprint. It takes time and effort to cultivate a community of engaged readers who are passionate about your books.

In conclusion, building a strong online presence is essential for children's authors looking to connect with young readers and boost book sales. By understanding your target audience, choosing the right social media platforms, crafting engaging content, and engaging with your audience consistently, you can create a compelling online presence that sets you apart in the competitive world of children's literature.

Embrace the power of social media and watch your children's book brand begin to make sales and your brand will start to make so many relationships you never expected.

CHAPTER 5:

CONNECTING WITH YOUNG READERS

In today's digital age, social media has become a powerful tool for authors to engage with their audience and promote their books. When it comes to marketing children's books, connecting with young readers through social media is essential.

By understanding the interests and behaviors of young audiences, authors can create meaningful connections that resonate with their readers.

One of the key strategies for connecting with young readers on social media is to create content that is not only entertaining but also educational and interactive. Children are drawn to content that is visually appealing, fun, and easy to understand.

Incorporating colorful images, engaging videos, and interactive posts can capture the attention of young readers and keep them interested in your books. Another important aspect of connecting with young readers on social media is to create a strong online presence.

This means maintaining active profiles on popular platforms such as Instagram, Facebook, Twitter, and TikTok.

By consistently sharing updates, behind-the-scenes content, and sneak peeks of upcoming books, authors can build a loyal following of young readers who are excited to engage with their favorite authors.

Engagement is key when it comes to connecting with young readers on social media. Responding to comments, hosting live Q&A sessions, and running interactive contests are effective ways to foster a sense of community and make young readers feel valued and appreciated.

By actively engaging with your audience, you can cultivate a dedicated fan base that will eagerly support your work and help spread the word about your books.

In addition to creating engaging content and fostering a strong online presence, it is important for authors to stay true to their brand and maintain authenticity when connecting with young readers on social media. Children are perceptive and can easily detect insincerity, so it is crucial to be genuine, transparent, and relatable in your interactions with young audiences.

By implementing these social media strategies and techniques, authors can effectively connect with young readers, build a loyal fan base, and ultimately drive book sales.

In the competitive world of children's literature, establishing a strong presence on social media is essential for authors looking to make a lasting impact and reach a wider audience of young readers. Embrace the magic of social media and unlock the potential to connect with young readers in ways that will inspire, entertain, and captivate their imaginations.

CHapTer 6:

BOOSTING BOOK SaLeS

In today's digital age, social media has become a powerful tool for authors to reach their target audience and increase book sales. The key to successfully leveraging social media for book marketing lies in understanding your audience and creating engaging content that resonates with them.

One of the first steps in boosting book sales through social media is to define your target audience. Children's book authors must understand the age group, interests, and preferences of their readers to tailor their content effectively.

By knowing your audience, you can create posts that are both entertaining and informative, capturing their attention and sparking their interest in your books.

Crafting engaging posts is essential to building a strong online presence and attracting followers. Visual content such as vibrant illustrations, book covers, and behind-the-scenes glimpses can help grab the attention of young readers scrolling through their feeds.

Interactive posts like polls, quizzes, and challenges can also encourage audience engagement and foster a sense of community around your books. Consistency is key when it comes to maintaining an active social media presence.

 Regularly posting updates, sharing sneak peeks of upcoming projects, and interacting with your audience through comments and messages can help keep your followers engaged and interested in your work.

By staying active on social media platforms, you can build a loyal fan base that eagerly anticipates your next book release.

Collaborating with influencers and bloggers in the children's literature niche can also help amplify your reach and boost book sales. Partnering with popular personalities who share your target audience can introduce your books to new readers and generate buzz around your brand.

By leveraging their platforms to promote your work, you can expand your online presence and attract a wider audience of potential book buyers.

In conclusion, social media offers a wealth of opportunities for children's book authors to connect with young readers and increase book sales. By understanding your audience, creating engaging content, and maintaining a consistent online presence, you can effectively promote your books and grow your brand in the competitive world of children's literature. Embrace the magic of social media marketing and watch your book sales soar to new heights.

CHAPTER 7: Captivating Audiences

Captivating audiences is key to building a loyal following and increasing book sales. To achieve this, authors must harness the magic of social media and create compelling content that resonates with young readers.

One of the first steps in captivating audiences through social media is understanding your target audience. Children's authors must tailor their content to appeal to the interests and preferences of their young readers.

By knowing what captivates children – whether it's colorful illustrations, interactive storytelling, or relatable characters – authors can create content that sparks curiosity and keeps young readers coming back for more.

Crafting engaging posts is essential for capturing the attention of young audiences on social media. Visual content, such as vibrant images and videos, can help bring your stories to life and make them more appealing to children.

Interactive posts, such as polls, quizzes, and challenges, can also encourage audience engagement and foster a sense of community among young readers. Building a strong online presence is crucial for children's authors looking to captivate audiences through social media.

By maintaining active profiles on popular platforms such as Instagram, Facebook, and TikTok, authors can reach a wider audience and connect with fans in real-time.

Consistent posting, regular interaction with followers, and showcasing behind-the-scenes glimpses of the creative process can all help build a loyal fan base and keep young readers excited about upcoming books.

In conclusion, captivating audiences through social media is a powerful strategy for children's authors to promote their books and connect with young readers. By understanding their target audience, crafting engaging posts, and building a strong online presence, authors can create a captivating online presence that resonates with young audiences and boosts book sales. Embrace the magic of social media and watch your children's book brand flourish in the digital landscape.

CHAPTER 8:

GROWING YOUR CHILDREN'S BOOK BRAND

With millions of active users, platforms like Facebook, Instagram, Twitter, and TikTok offer a vast potential audience for your children's books. By harnessing the power of social media, you can create a strong online presence, engage with your readers, and ultimately increase your book sales.

Crafting engaging posts is key to capturing the attention of young audiences. Visual content, such as eye-catching graphics and videos, tends to perform the best on social media. Consider creating interactive posts that encourage likes, shares, and comments from your followers.

By sparking conversations and fostering a sense of community around your books, you can cultivate a loyal fan base that will support your brand in the long run.

Building a consistent and cohesive online presence is crucial for establishing your children's book brand. Your social media profiles should reflect the tone and style of your books, creating a seamless experience for your audience. Color palettes, logo design, and having a cohesive theme to your brand is one of the most important things you can do to market yourself and your book. Part of your brand is your website, logo, colors, images, and content you produce. Make sure all of your content is representing you and your brand.

Use your platforms to showcase your writing journey, behind-the-scenes glimpses, and upcoming projects to keep your readers engaged and invested in your work. Engaging with your audience is key to building a strong connection with young readers. Respond to comments, messages, and feedback promptly to show your appreciation for their support.

Consider hosting live events, Q&A sessions, or book readings on social media to interact with your fans in real time. By making your readers feel valued and involved, you can cultivate a loyal following that will champion your books to others. In the competitive world of children's literature, standing out from the crowd is essential.

By utilizing social media effectively, you can showcase your unique voice and storytelling style to a global audience. With strategic planning, creativity, and consistency, you can grow your children's book brand and make a lasting impact in the hearts and minds of young readers worldwide. Don't miss out on this essential resource for authors aiming to make a splash in the world of children's literature.

CHapTer 9:
MakinG a SPLaSH in CHiLDren's LiTeraTure

In the vast ocean of children's literature, making a splash requires more than just writing a captivating story. It's about diving into the world of marketing and leveraging the power of social media to connect with young readers and propel your book to success.

In this chapter, we will explore the essential strategies and tactics that can help children's authors create waves in the competitive market.

One of the first steps in making a splash in children's literature is to establish a strong online presence. Social media platforms such as Instagram, Facebook, Twitter, and TikTok offer valuable opportunities to engage with your audience and build a community around your book. By creating profiles that reflect your brand and sharing content that resonates with your target demographic, you can cultivate a loyal following of young readers and their parents.

Crafting engaging posts is key to capturing the attention of your audience in the fast-paced world of social media. Visual content, such as eye-catching graphics, book trailers, and videos, can help bring your book to life and spark interest among potential readers.

Additionally, interactive features like polls, quizzes, and live streams can foster a sense of connection and interactivity that keeps followers coming back for more.

Collaborating with influencers and bloggers who cater to children's literature can also amplify your reach and introduce your book to new audiences. By partnering with individuals who have a strong following among young readers, you can leverage their influence to generate buzz and drive sales.

Offering exclusive content, hosting giveaways, or organizing virtual events can further incentivize influencers to promote your book to their followers.

Building a community around your children's book is not just about promoting your work—it's about fostering genuine connections with your audience. Engage with your followers by responding to comments, asking for feedback, and sharing behind-the-scenes glimpses into your writing process. By creating a dialogue with your readers, you can cultivate a sense of loyalty and enthusiasm that turns casual fans into devoted advocates for your book.

In the competitive landscape of children's literature, standing out requires creativity, persistence, and a strategic approach to marketing. By harnessing the power of social media and implementing targeted strategies to connect with young readers, children's authors can make a splash that resonates far and wide.

Don't underestimate the impact of a well-crafted social media presence—it could be the key to unlocking success in the world of children's literature.

CHAPTER 10: CONCLUSION

In the fast-paced world of children's literature, connecting with young readers and standing out in a crowded market requires more than just a great story. It demands a strategic approach to marketing that harnesses the power of social media to engage audiences, build relationships, and ultimately drive book sales. "Children's Book Marketing Magic: Social Media Strategies for Children's Authors" has taken you on a journey through the essential tools and techniques needed to succeed in this dynamic landscape.

Throughout this book, we've explored the art of crafting compelling posts that resonate with children and parents alike. We've delved into the importance of creating a consistent and authentic online presence that reflects your unique voice and brand.

By understanding the nuances of different social media platforms and tailoring your content to suit each one, you can effectively reach your target audience and cultivate a loyal following.

But successful book promotion doesn't stop at creating engaging content. It also involves fostering meaningful connections with your readers, engaging in conversations, and listening to feedback.

By actively participating in online communities, responding to comments, and soliciting input from your audience, you can build trust and loyalty that will pay dividends in the long run.

As we conclude our exploration of social media strategies for children's authors, remember that the key to success lies in authenticity, consistency, and creativity. By staying true to your brand, maintaining a regular posting schedule, and experimenting with different formats and approaches, you can unlock the full potential of social media as a marketing tool.

So, whether you're a seasoned author looking to revitalize your children's book brand or a newcomer eager to make a splash in the industry, "Children's Book Marketing Magic" is your go-to resource for navigating the complex world of book promotion.

Armed with the insights and strategies outlined in this book, you have the tools you need to captivate audiences, grow your readership, and make a lasting impact in the hearts and minds of young readers everywhere.

Embrace the magic of social media, and watch your children's book brand soar all while boosting sales, and getting your book into the hands of the right audience.

ABOUT

KeriAnne N. Jelinek

FOUNDER | CEO | AUTHOR | ILLUSTRATOR | CHILDREN'S BOOK CONSULTANT
BOOK MARKETING STRATEGIST | ENTREPRENEUR | PUBLISHER

KeriAnne N. Jelinek is a highly accomplished figure in the world of children's literature, distinguished as a best-selling author, astute publisher, children's book marketing expert, and sought-after book consultant. As the CEO & Founder of Sloth Dreams Books & Publishing, LLC, she has steered the creation and self-publication of an impressive catalog of over 180 children's books since January 2022, marking a significant imprint on the literary landscape. Her dedication to the craft extends beyond writing, encompassing roles as an illustrator, editor, and cover designer, showcasing her comprehensive understanding of the publishing industry.

In addition to her prowess as an author and publisher, KeriAnne has demonstrated her expertise as a book marketer, making notable appearances on various media platforms, including podcasts, radio stations, TV, and news outlets, both domestically and internationally. Her podcast, "Sloths Love to Read," has garnered a substantial global following, reaching over 80 countries monthly. Her books have appeared in bookstores and libraries around the world. Ms. Jelinek also runs a children's YouTube Channel that features books from around the globe. She is a strong supporter of children's self-published authors, and has promoted over 200 authors on her social media platforms and on her podcasts. In addition, Ms. Jelinek, has written a self-publishing book entitled "The Magic Launch: Unlock the Secrets to Self-Publishing & Grow Rich" and has created her own trademarked method, called "The Magic Launch Method". Her courses, coaching, consultation, and publishing services can be found helping authors worldwide.

KeriAnne's literary achievements are highlighted by consistent #1 rankings in Top New Releases and Top Best-Seller categories, a testament to the quality and appeal of her creations. Notably, her work "Ukraine: My Country" gained recognition on Spin Chat Radio in the UK and numerous radio stations across Pennsylvania. She is an active participant in author's forums within Pennsylvania and has graced several podcasts, including "The Homeschool Advantage Podcast" as a featured expert and guest. Her books have been featured in magazines and children's companies around the world. Her books can be found in libraries, schools, churches, and homes around the world.

Her literary offerings are widely accessible, available on prominent platforms such as Amazon, Barnes & Noble, Kobo, Wal-Mart, Google Books, Ingram Spark, and more, ensuring a global reach. KeriAnne's diverse professional background, including over 25 years as a music educator and professional performer, opera singer, pianist, and vocal coach, adds a unique dimension to her work. She holds a Bachelor's Degree in Vocal Performance, K-12 Music Certification, and K-6 Elementary Education Certification.

KeriAnne currently resides in Pennsylvania, where she finds solace in writing, reading, playing the piano, directing music, owning and operating her company, and teaching. Her transition from a successful teaching career to the world of educational children's book writing stems from a deep passion for nurturing creativity and providing meaningful educational experiences. A diagnosed individual with Asperger's Autism, her distinctive perspective enriches her writing, imbuing it with creativity and relatability to a wide audience. With a wealth of ideas for children's books, KeriAnne is excited about the professional entrepreneurial journey that lies ahead, fueled by her love for nature, art, music, business, and writing. She resides with her husband and daughter, and their Russian Blue cat, Sir Mackerel Blue.

www.ingramcontent.com/pod-product-compliance
Lightning Source LLC
La Vergne TN
LVHW031235190726
843491LV00010B/3010